TYRONE

THE ROAD TO GLORY

BARRY FLYNN

PHOTOGRAPHY BY JIM DUNNE

Appletree Press

To Dermot
& Kathleen
Best Wishes

Barry Flynn

To Katrina, Meabh and Deirbhile
And the Gaels of Tyrone

First published in 2008 by
Appletree Press Ltd
The Old Potato Station
14 Howard Street South
Belfast BT7 1AP

Tel: +44 (0) 28 90 243074
Fax: +44 (0) 28 90 246756

Website: www.appletree.ie
Email: reception@appletree.ie

Copyright © Appletree Press, 2008
Text © Barry Flynn, 2008
Photographs © Jim Dunne, 2008
Additional photography by Sportsfile (pp24-31)

A catalogue record for this book is available from the British Library.

TYRONE - THE ROAD TO GLORY

ISBN: 978 1 84758 137 2

Desk & Marketing Editor: Jean Brown
Editorial Work: Jim Black
Designer: Stuart Wilkinson
Production Manager: Paul McAvoy

9 8 7 6 5 4 3 2 1

AP 3620

CONTENTS

"Tír Eoghain Abu!"

TYRONE PROVE THE CRITICS WRONG – AGAIN

Just after five o'clock on Sunday 21st September 2008, Tyrone's victorious captain Brian Dooher climbed the steps of the Hogan Stand in Croke Park. The Clan na nGael man made steady progress upwards to where the great and the good of Irish society awaited: but the only thing that Dooher could see though was the gleaming glory of Ireland's most famous trophy – the Sam Maguire Cup. Behind him, bedecked in their red and white, stood the heaving mass that was the loyal Tyrone support, while a solid wall of Gardai kept good order. The rest of the Tyrone squad, manager Mickey Harte and his backroom team, all watched Dooher's progress from below the presentation box. The moment was almost there as President of the GAA, Nickey Brennan, greeted the Tyrone captain warmly and lifted his microphone to begin.

This is an honour that every Gaelic footballer can only dream about. Brian Dooher, however, had for the second time captained Tyrone to victory in the All-Ireland Senior Football Final. He, and his team, had become living legends in Gaelic Football and in every corner of the O'Neill County. Soon, the ground erupted as the Cup was presented. Dooher held it aloft and savoured every second of the glory. It was a sweet, sweet moment in the proud history of Tyrone football. They had won their third All-Ireland since 2003 and from Dromore to Dungannon, Strabane to Sion Mills, Carrickmore to Croke Park the party was just beginning.

Below the Hogan Stand in the Kerry dressing room, the silence was punctured by the distant roars of the Tyrone supporters. The favourites had lost – fairly and squarely – to their Northern opponents – again! The majority of the written media had placed Kerry on a pedestal and, in theory, they only had to turn up to claim their 36th title. On the pitch before the game, GAA pundit Martin Carney told RTE Commentator Ger Canning that he fancied Kerry by 'five points': when, oh when, would they learn? Never, ever, write off the men of Tyrone. History had proved this point time and time again.

The evidence was there for all to see. Mickey Harte's men had consistently proved to be the better team whenever Tyrone met the men from the Kingdom. In 2003, the two teams had met in a semi-final that changed forever the game of Gaelic Football. As massive underdogs, Tyrone went at Kerry with a ferocity that unsettled them greatly. Tackling, crowding and winning possession were the by-words of Tyrone's play that day. However, it was character, teamwork and determination – with no shortage of skill – that were crucial to Tyrone's victory in Croke Park. Some pundits called it 'the blanket defence' or in one famous case 'puke football', but, in hindsight, that was just a case of sour grapes. That September, Tyrone under the inspirational Peter Canavan triumphed over Armagh in the first all-Northern final. Harte used Canavan to great effect in that game, by taking him off and bringing him back on to lift both the team and, crucially, the crowd. One incident, however, displayed the determination of the Tyrone side. With seconds remaining and Armagh trailing, the ball broke to their key marksman Stevie McDonnell, who had only one thing in mind as he closed in on goal. He was odds-on to score and deprive Tyrone of victory until the inspirational Conor Gormley found that last drop of energy and went full length to block his shot – the ground erupted and Tyrone were home. In Harte's first year as manager, his team won the National Football League, the Ulster Championship and then defeated the reigning champions in the All Ireland Final. It was too good to be true. It was.

It is said that adversity builds character in teams. In this respect, the Gaelic footballers of Tyrone have endured much tragic adversity in their struggle to be Ireland's top team. On Tuesday, 2nd March 2004, Tyrone and Ireland was shaken to the core by the news of the death of Tyrone star Cormac McAnallen. The twenty-four-year-old schoolteacher stood for everything that is great about the Gaelic Athletic Association. He was a joy to behold on a playing field, a dedicated leader, an inspiration and a role model. He had just been made captain of the Tyrone side and had lifted the Dr McKenna Cup a short time before his death. He was truly remarkable and who knows what heights he would have achieved in his future years. His death was attributed to Sudden Cardiac Arrest and his passing touched everyone. It wasn't the first tragic episode that had affected Tyrone football in recent times. In 1997, Paul McGirr from the Dromore club was playing minor football for Tyrone in the Championship against Armagh when he sustained a fatal injury and died on the way to hospital. That 1997 minor team included Cormac McAnallen and was managed at the time by Mickey Harte. Both players have never been far from the thoughts of those associated with the GAA in Tyrone as the county had found the spirit and inspiration to rise above cruel adversity.

In 2004, Tyrone's defence of their title began with an easy 14-point victory over Derry in the preliminary round of the Ulster Championship at Clones. All but one of the champion's points came from open play. In midfield, Sean Cavanagh ruled the roost while Kevin Hughes and Brian Dooher ran the Derry defence a merry dance. It seemed to be business as usual for the Red Hands, and Fermanagh were dispatched in Clones by 1-13 to 12 points in the first round proper of the Championship. In the semi-final, it was a tired Tyrone team who were defeated by Donegal by 1-11 to nine points in front of 34,000 spectators at Clones. Condemned to the 'scenic route' known as the Qualifiers, Tyrone eased past Down in Newry and then went to Croke Park in July and beat Galway by an impressive eight points. Peter Canavan made a welcome return to the side, but it was a goal by Brian McGuigan after 11 minutes that set up the victory. Owen Mulligan was in sparkling form as he notched up five points, while Stephen O'Neill chipped in with four. However, the campaign ended in disappointment in the quarter-final when Mayo

proved too good on the day and won by 16 points to 1-9. Hopes of retaining the title had been dashed, but it had been a truly traumatic year. In the final that year, Kerry found their class to defeat easily the challenge of Mayo. The Tyrone team vowed to rise again in 2005.

The following year, Tyrone opened their campaign with a 1-13 to 1-6 win over Down in Newry. The first meeting of Tyrone and Cavan in the Ulster semi-final clash at Clones was to end in a draw. However, the Red Hand men went into overdrive in the replay and thumped the Breffnimen: a serious message had been sent out regarding Tyrone's All-Ireland intentions. Three first-half goals from Peter Canavan, Stephen O'Neill and Philip Jordan set up an eagerly anticipated Ulster Final against Armagh at Croke Park. The final went to a replay and in a very scrappy game Armagh took the honours and again Tyrone headed to the Qualifiers.

Monaghan did not put up a fight as Tyrone saw off their challenge in early August to set up a quarter-final date with Dublin on Saturday 13th August. The game in front of a packed Headquarters went one way and then the other. Trailing by five points at the break, Tyrone fought like tigers. In the fiftieth minute, Eoin Mulligan scored 'that goal' and left the spectators in awe. It took an extra-time equalising point from Dublin's Tomas Quinn to force the game to a replay. Tyrone, however, were on the up. The replay the following week was Tyrone's and Mulligan again was the hero as he hit 1-7 of Tyrone's 2-18, while Dublin trailed behind with 1-14. Armagh (again) waited in the semi-final.

The semi-final clash with Armagh was as tense as it was close, with Stephen O'Neill's penalty helping Tyrone to a 1-4 to 0-5 lead after a frantic first-half. It took a last-minute Peter Canavan free to give the victory to the Red Hands and set up the tie with reigning champions Kerry on 25th September. Again, the pundits wrote-off Mickey Harte's team by making Kerry hot-favourites. Again they were to be proved wrong.

In the final, Tyrone were superb as they outplayed the men from the Kingdom. In his last game for his county, Peter Canavan was coolness personified as he collected a neat pass from Eoin Mulligan to slide home Tyrone's goal in their 1-16 to 2-10 victory. It took ten games in all – including three replays – but the O'Neill County were once again the team of the moment. The win was duly dedicated to the memory of Cormac McAnallen. An emotional Mickey Harte paid tribute to his former star player:

"When Cormac was made Tyrone captain he said he did not want to leave it with just one All-Ireland – and he hasn't. It has been a long hard road; we played ten games and this is just a wonderful day for the county."

For whatever reason, 2006 was a very poor year in All-Ireland terms for Tyrone. On 28th May, Derry came to Omagh: by the break they had registered six points and kept Tyrone scoreless. Kevin Hughes was sent-off for an off-the-ball incident and the game as a contest was ended by a goal on 48 minutes by Derry's Enda Muldoon which ended any hopes of a comeback. Tyrone lost by 1-8 to five points and thousands had left Healy Park in disappointment well before the final whistle. The Qualifiers provided Tyrone with a tricky tie against an improving Louth in Navan in June. The game was a classic which went to a replay after extra time. Owen Mulligan hit two goals within a minute as Tyrone led 2-7 to 0-6 at half-time. Louth though came out and brought the game to the champions after the break. It took two points from the inspirational Mulligan to tie the game and send them back to Omagh.

It was again a nervy Tyrone side that appeared on the pitch at Healy Park for the replay. However, they did just about enough to warrant a five-point victory – at a price. Ryan Mellon was sent-off and both Collie Holmes and Conor Gormley suffered injuries. It was a weakened Tyrone side that was to lose to Laois by nine points to six on 8th July. The knives were sharpened for the Tyrone team as they departed the Championship, a shadow of the team which had scaled the heights ten months previously. As I said earlier, never, ever write off Tyrone. Kerry showed no mercy to Mayo in that year's final as they triumphed on a 4-15 to 3-5 scoreline.

In 2007, Tyrone retained the Ulster title after a close win over Fermanagh and a fabulous display in the semi-final when Donegal were truly 'put to the sword'. Brian Dooher was immense as he inspired Tyrone to a 1-6 to 1-3 interval lead with Colm McCullagh

dispatching Tyrone's goal from the penalty spot. After the break, Raymond Mulgrew hit Tyrone's second goal. Donegal's abysmal display was further compounded when Colm McFadden was sent off for a punch on Dooher. In the final, 36,000 fans packed Clones to see Tyrone hold off a determined challenge from Monaghan to take the Cup. However, with Ulster conquered, Tyrone set their sights on the bigger prize in September. It was not to be. In the quarter-final Meath were to triumph on a 1-13 to 2-8 score. Brian Dooher was unfit, replaced by Enda McGinley, but Tyrone had a very 'off day'. Sean Cavanagh hit a superb goal but Tyrone trailed ten points to 1-5 at the break. Things looked up as Mulligan scored a opportunist goal but Graham Geraghty – with a goal and two points – inspired the Royals to victory, despite a late onslaught from Tyrone. Again, Tyrone had fallen short. The pundits asked: was time running out for the team that Mickey Harte built? In the 2007 final, Kerry took the honours with an easy win over neighbours Cork. The year 2008 would see them go for 'three-in-a-row' and who, if anyone, would stop them? Things, however, are never as straightforward as that – especially when a team such as Tyrone has a point to prove.

The 2008 Ulster Championship began for Tyrone on Sunday 8th June when Down came to Omagh in the first round. Tyrone enjoyed a great start: goals from Colm McCullagh and Sean Cavanagh saw them lead 2-3 to 0-2 after 17 minutes. Down upped their game and Benny Coulter found the net; by the fiftieth minute they were leading after Ambrose Rodgers got their second goal. The match ebbed and flowed. Tyrone led by a point and were on their way to victory only for Down to level with a Paul McComiskey free late on, which meant that a replay was required in Newry.

The replay on the following Saturday evening was to end in bitter defeat for Tyrone. After a thrilling encounter, Down were to triumph by a single point: 1-19 to twenty-one points after extra time. Yet again, Benny Coulter was the key man as he fired home the game's only goal. The Red Hands fought well and led by single figures at the break but Down dominated the early stages of the second half, and soon led by four points. Tyrone dug deep and the game went to extra-time and Down shaded the result, to the delight of their thousands of fans. Tyrone had fallen short in Ulster, but it was a poor pundit who would write them off. However, the team – and Mickey Harte in particular – came in for a lot of criticism after the Down defeat. The bookmakers lengthened their odds on a Tyrone All-Ireland win in 2008. The defeat in Ulster was not the end of the world for Tyrone. They had class – that does not vanish overnight; they had determination and, most importantly, they had spirit. It was a case of battening down the hatches and getting on with the job in hand – to reclaim the Sam Maguire Cup in 2008.

The well-worn route of the Qualifiers now beckoned for Tyrone. On 19th July, they re-entered the fray, and enjoyed a comfortable win over Louth in Drogheda. Tyrone soon got into their stride. Through points from Martin Penrose, Tommy McGuigan and Sean Cavanagh they opened up an early three-point lead. Louth were soon level but this fact only inspired Tyrone to greater things and they took the 'Wee County' apart for the rest of the game. They were fast, they were accurate and a goal from Enda McGinley ended the game as a contest. Still, the pundits said, it was only Louth! Tyrone won by 1-18 to 1-10 and they were back in the hunt.

Westmeath came to Omagh on 26th July and put up a brave performance. In truth, Tyrone made hard work of the game and Westmeath had two men sent off in the second half. Tommy McGuigan top-scored for Tyrone with six points and despite their disadvantage, Westmeath almost stole the game when Dessie Dolan missed a fabulous goal chance five minutes from the end. The game was won by fourteen points to 1-7 by Tyrone and they were progressing slowly but surely. Still, very few outside the O'Neill County reckoned that they would progress much further. Oh ye of little faith!

On 2nd August, Tyrone showed character to come back from three points down to beat Mayo in the third round of the Qualifiers. Again, the performance was not a vintage one but Tyrone did enough to win. Trailing by 1-7 to seven points early in the second half the Red Hands hit a purple patch, hitting six points in a row to take command. Sean Cavanagh was in fabulous form and hit four points, while Enda McGinley put in a man-of-the-match display. The Championship was

down to eight teams. Tyrone were still there, while their rivals Down had crashed out. Who would be next up for the ever-improving side? The answer: Dublin – and sure that was only a formality for the Dubs, according to the pundits in the know.

Dare I say that the Tyrone display against Dublin was one of the most emphatic victories of this decade? It was a joy to behold for Tyrone fans as they triumphed by 3-14 to 1-8 – it was in fact more one-sided than the scoreline suggests. Sean Cavanagh and Joe McMahon hit the net during the first half and Davy Harte grabbed a third after the break to secure a semi-final date against Wexford. Tyrone moved and passed with intelligence as the Dublin team could only watch as mere shadows. The streets around Croke were a sea of blue-shirted Dubliners well before the final whistle as their team's failings had been exposed brutally. The result was 'a shock' they said in the Dublin papers – but Mickey Harte and his squad knew better.

Wexford – who had regrouped following a hammering from Dublin in the Leinster Final – were to be Tyrone's semi-final opponents. The dream of the Model County men was not to be, as the Red Hands asserted themselves on the day to win by twenty-three points to 1-14, with all but five of Tyrone's scores coming from play. Tyrone played some excellent attacking football as they eased into a nine-point lead during the opening period. The match result was never then in doubt as the Red Hands closed out the game.

There is only one team to beat in an All-Ireland Football Final: Kerry. The men from the Kingdom duly saw off rivals Cork in their semi-final to set up the final that everybody wanted – Tyrone v Kerry on 21st September. The search for tickets was on in the heartland of the O'Neill County. Soon the streets and towns were bedecked in the red-and-white colours of the team, and the talk in the shops and bars was of football and tickets. They were calling it the battle of the decade, the match to settle the argument: "just who are the team of the 'Noughties'?"

The media questioned Tyrone's ability to upset the Kerry forwards. The 'Twin Towers' of Donaghy and Walsh would be too much for their backs. Tyrone were not the team that they once were, so they said, and, sure, weren't Kerry certain for three titles in a row? The Kingdom had the game as good as in the bag. Yet, as everyone with a titter of wit knows, a game is won nowhere but on the pitch – predictions of the demise of Tyrone were a bit premature.

At 3.30pm on All Ireland Final day, referee Maurice Deegan threw the ball in to signal the start of the game: the time for talking was over. The game flowed from end to end, with the lead changing hands seven times before 'Gooch' Cooper nudged Kerry 0-8 to 0-7 ahead before the break.

Cometh the hour, Cometh the men! After 22 seconds of the second half, Tommy McGuigan scrambled home the game's only goal. The ground erupted and now the Tyrone fans could believe. Both Dooher and Canavan started to do their 'stuff' and the Red Hands soon were ahead by three points.

Kerry fought back. Cooper gave them the lead, but Tyrone were made of sterner stuff. Both teams went at it like two heavyweights slugging it out toe-to-toe in the ring. Cavanagh burst through again to put Tyrone 1-12 to 0-14 ahead. It was to be a crucial score. Kerry were rattled: they had run out if ideas – there was no Plan B.

However, Pascal McConnell was called upon to deny a certain goal from Declan O'Sullivan's low shot. Back came the Red Hands to finish the job. Enda McGinley hit a point, then Hughes and finally Colm Cavanagh secured the day with the final point at the death. Game, set and match.

The final whistle was greeted with glee by Tyrone people in every corner of the world. They had proved everyone wrong to take glory for the third time in the 'Noughties'. They deserved it. They displayed spirit, class and determination in abundance. They feared nobody, and thrived as the year unfolded. This 'Sam Maguire' business is becoming quite a habit for Tyrone on the steps of the Hogan Stand in September.

This book is dedicated to the people of Tyrone. To the men and women whose tireless dedication over the decades turned dreams into the miracles of 2003, 2005 and 2008. And to those who will bring glory to the Red Hand County in future years.

Tír Eoghain Abu!
Barry Flynn

THE ROAD TO GLORY

Sunday, June 8 - Omagh

Ulster SFC Quarter-Final

Tyrone 2-8 Down 2-8

Left: Sunday 8th June was a fine summer's day at Healy Park in Omagh as Tyrone faced the men from Down in the Ulster Senior Football Quarter-Final.

The Red Hands went in as hot-favourites to see off the challenge of Ross Carr's men. In the eighth minute Colm McCullagh found the net to put daylight between the sides. Ten minutes later, Tyrone registered a second goal (Left) when Sean Cavanagh, who was filling the full-forward spot, crashed the ball to the net past the despairing dives of Down goalkeeper Brendan McVeigh and defender Aidan Carr. By that stage, Tyrone led 2-3 to two points, and a home win seemed a certainty. Time and time again in the first twenty minutes of the game, the Down defence was ripped apart, but then came the comeback. By the break, Tyrone led by 2-4 to 1-3 with Benny Coulter having raised the green flag for the Mourne men. In the fiftieth minute, Ambrose Rodgers punched to the net and it was 'game on'. Tyrone were struggling but they hit the front through points from Dooher and Hughes: a last-gasp free from Down's Paul McComiskey levelled the game and secured a replay in Newry.

Above: The joy is evident of the face of Sean Cavanagh as he turns to greet his teammates after he had scored.

By this stage, Tyrone were coasting but Ross Carr's men had a few surprises in store for the Red Hands.

Right: Kevin Hughes watches as his shot comes agonisingly off the crossbar during the drawn game in Omagh.

Hughes was brought on as an early sub for Enda McGinley in midfield, but was then moved up to the full-forward berth. He scored a point in the dying seconds of the game, only for a well-executed free from Down's Paul McComiskey to level matters. Hughes was an important member of the successful Tyrone team in 2003, and took the coveted Man of the Match award for his performance in the final. He travelled to Australia in 2005 and missed out on a second All-Ireland medal, making a comeback in a Dr McKenna Cup game against Armagh in January 2006. In the 2008 final, it was a shot from Hughes – which Kerry goalkeeper Diarmuid Murphy parried – that set up the game's only goal for Tommy McGuigan just after the break.

Right: A beardless Martin Penrose almost finds the net in the early stages of the Ulster Championship clash with Down in Omagh.

The corner-forward's effort was inches away, as his low shot went agonisingly wide past Brendan McVeigh's post. Tyrone tore at the Down defence in the opening twenty minutes and Colm McCullagh fired home their first goal in the eighth minute, with Sean Cavanagh adding a second ten minutes later.

Penrose was instrumental in the build-up to McCullagh's goal when he picked out Brian McGuigan – who was starting his first Championship game since 2005 – who then found McCullagh, who hit a left-foot shot past Brendan McVeigh. Indeed, it was a flicked pass by Penrose that allowed Cavanagh to add the second goal.

In the second half, Penrose added a point for Tyrone and could have won the game, but his late effort crashed off the crossbar. Down custodian Brendan McVeigh made his inter-county Championship debut in 2005 – again at Omagh against Tyrone. That game was played in a torrential downpour and saw the Red Hands victorious on a 1-13 to 1-6 scoreline.

MATCH 2

Saturday, June 14 - Newry

Ulster SFC Quarter-Final Replay

Down 1-19 Tyrone 0-21

Left: Ciaran Gourley and Down's Liam Doyle race for the ball while Dan McCartan watches proceedings in the background.

Saturday night football has been an undoubted success in Newry with the redeveloped Páirc Esler hosting some large attendances in recent years. In 2007 Meath brought a massive support to the venue and came away with a deserved win. For the Down and Tyrone replay, a crowd of 18,272 crammed into the ground. The match was delayed for 15 minutes as traffic problems in Newry meant that many thousands were still outside the ground at throw-in time. Down's victory was greeted by the home fans with great rejoicing, although Armagh then beat the Mournemen on their way to reclaiming the Ulster title.

Above: Despite the efforts of Brendan McVeigh, Joe McMahon goes agonisingly close during the replay against Down.

Right: Philip Jordan shows the pain of defeat in Newry.

Down football and its supporters have seen many false dawns since the glory days of 1991 and 1994, when 'Sam' found a second home in the Mourne County. Their supporters left Páirc Esler after the win over Tyrone on a high, thinking that 2008 could just be their year. As the old adage goes: you don't win titles in June. If you could pinpoint a moment Tyrone's season was to change for the better, it was probably at the final whistle in Newry. A truly titanic struggle had seen Down victorious and, for Tyrone, it was time to regroup. Enda McGinley had missed that game through injury and his return later in the season was crucial for Tyrone. The Red Hands evolved into champions and for Down the stark truth was that their victory in Newry was the highpoint of their season.

The 'Greatest' Muhammad Ali once observed that 'No one knows what to say in the loser's locker room'. It is a painful experience to be knocked out in the early stages of the Ulster Championship, and a five-week lay-off until the start of the Qualifiers can damage a team's morale. The All-Ireland Qualifiers – or the backdoor system – has its fans and critics. The system was introduced in 2001 to allow a second chance in the All-Ireland series for those counties knocked out of their Provincial series. That year, Galway became the first football side to win an All-Ireland through the Qualifiers. Tyrone won the All-Irelands of 2005 and 2008 through the 'backdoor' system, while the 2008 Ulster Champions Armagh crashed out to Wexford in the All-Ireland quarter-final.

MATCH 3

Saturday, July 19 - Drogheda

All-Ireland SFC Qualifiers Round 1

Louth 1-10 Tyrone 1-18

Left: The Iron Fist in the Leather Glove

They call Gordon Brown 'The Clunking Fist': perhaps this nickname could be applied also to Louth goalkeeper Stuart Reynolds, as Brian Dooher's face tells the tale of this collision. Dooher led his troops into the fray against Louth and they escaped unscathed. Louth insisted on playing the game in Drogheda, an all-ticket affair limited to a relatively small 4,500 crowd. After the game, John Campbell, the GAA correspondent for the *Belfast Telegraph* wrote 'Tyrone are lurking among the bushes, ready to spring another big push for All-Ireland honours' – how right he was to be proved. Tyrone scored at ease with Colm McCullagh hitting five, Sean Cavanagh four and Brian McGuigan weighing in with three points. The workhorse Brian Dooher, surprisingly, finished the game with only one point to his name.

Above: Enda McGinley turns away to celebrate after scoring Tyrone's goal in the thirtieth minute of the game against Louth.

It was a case of déjà vu for both teams – and Enda McGinley – as in 2006 the sides met in the Qualifiers. It took two matches to separate the sides, with McGinley finding the net in the replay.

The first game in 2006 was an enthralling affair that ended in a draw – 2-16 each after extra-time. Tyrone trailed as the game entered its final stages, but through Eoin Mulligan – who grabbed a remarkable personal tally of 2-6 – a draw was salvaged. In the replay, Tyrone came out on top – 1-12 to 1-7 – with the vital goal again coming from Enda McGinley. It was evident from early on in the 2008 clash that Louth would not pose the threat they had two years previously. Louth's odyssey in the Leinster Championship ended at Croke Park on Sunday 8th June: Dublin proved to be too good on the day and romped home in front of 55,000 spectators on a 1-22 to 0-12 scoreline.

Above: Tyrone were on fire during this game and Tommy McGuigan is seen racing in on goal pursued by Louth's Jamie Carr.

Had he scored, it would have been a most spectacular individual goal for McGuigan, but he was to drag his shot just wide of the post. Minutes later Martin Penrose was to miss another excellent goal chance but Tyrone's domination was total. Whilst Louth football has made progress in recent years, Tyrone were at least two classes above their opponents on the night.

The 'Wee County' have not made a Leinster Final appearance since 1960, when they lost to Offaly. During the last century, Louth won three All-Ireland Senior titles – in 1910, 1912 and 1957. In 1957, The county defeated Dublin in the 1957 Leinster final and, in September, beat Cork to lift the Sam Maguire Cup. Their captain that year was the renowned musician and singer Dermot O'Brien, who sadly passed away in 2007.

Above: Michael McGee surges past Louth's John Neary in Drogheda.

The 'Man from the Lough' is the nickname for Mickey McGee who won All-Ireland Senior medals with Tyrone in 2003 and 2005. From the Loughmacrory club, McGee was a member of the successful Minor side that claimed national honours under Mickey Harte in 1998. He soon graduated to the Under-21 county side and added two further winner's medals in 2000 and 2001. In 2005, he started the final against Kerry as a corner-back. However, plagued by a shoulder injury in recent times, he was not a regular starter in the side in 2008. Mickey was also known as one of the 'Beardy Boys' – the name given to several of the panel that began to sport beards in the aftermath of the defeat against Down. By the day of the final in September, the craze had caught on, as many supporters turned up in Croke Park with false whiskers in honour of their team.

Above: Stuart Reynolds and Mick Fanning of Louth in action against Sean Cavanagh.

After the defeat to Down, Tyrone had a lot of time on their hands. Given the nature of the Qualifier – or the back door – competition. A period of thirty-five days had elapsed from the defeat in Newry until the Red Hands took the field to face Louth in Drogheda. The murmurs of discontent regarding Tyrone's defeat had been aired by some of their supporters and included calls for the resignation of Mickey Harte. Many Tyrone players described the work carried out during that break as some of the hardest and most intense that they had ever experienced. If the supporters were hurt by the Down defeat, so were the players, manager and everyone involved with the Tyrone set-up were hurt also. Sean Cavanagh described that defeat to Down as 'the worst moment in the senior careers of most of the current Tyrone squad and leaves them with huge personal challenges that they never thought, after winning two All-Irelands, they would have to meet.' He also described the treatment of Mickey Harte as 'crazy' and added that 'whenever the ball is thrown in it's the responsibility of the players on the field'. The pressure was most definitely on Mickey Harte and his players in Drogheda – but they delivered in style.

Saturday, July 26 – Omagh

All-Ireland SFC Qualifier Round 2

Tyrone 0-14 Westmeath 1-7

Left: There are literally ninety seconds until throw-in and all the preparations are over.

The Tyrone side are now totally focussed as they stand to attention for the national anthem. It has been well-documented that total respect for the anthem has been part of the Tyrone philosophy - be that learning the words or staying together as a group until the final line has been sung. It's all part of the preparation and routine to get the team into top gear before the throw-in. Westmeath came to Omagh on Saturday 26th July and, despite home advantage, Mickey Harte was not writing off the side that had lost narrowly to Dublin in the Leinster Championship semi-final. By half-time in the game, Westmeath led 1-5 to 0-6 and they increased their lead to three when Martin Flanagan added a further point. Back came the Red Hands – points from Davy Harte, Tommy McGuigan and Enda McGinley with two squared the game. The Midlanders then lost two players – Healy and Harte – to red cards after they had become involved with Brian Dooher. Tyrone secured the game with points from Dooher, Damien McCaul and Ryan Mellon, but it was a scrappy affair as Tyrone progressed. They were winning and that's all that counted: the big performances could wait for Croke Park.

Right: The Ballet of Healy Park on 26th July.

Sean Cavanagh arrives into the action in a rather unorthodox manner, as full-back Justin McMahon provides some symmetry for the all-action picture. In the background is Westmeath full-forward Denis Glennon, who had just flicked the ball on for his colleague Michael Ennis to score the opening goal of the game. This came after thirty minutes and, not surprisingly, Cavanagh would be stretchered off after this challenge to be replaced by his brother Colm. In the prolonged delay before Cavanagh's departure, Mickey Harte called his team into a huddle to try to reorganise and settle the side, which had lost the lead after going four points to one up earlier in the game. A crowd of just 8,000 was to witness Tyrone's comeback in the second half. Afterwards, Mickey Harte said he was 'relieved more than delighted' by the win, and had Westmeath's marksman Dessie Dolan been able to finish to the net two late goal chances, then Tyrone's season would have ended that afternoon.

Left: Ouch!

If you study this picture carefully, you will note how lucky Sean Cavanagh was not to have done himself a more serious injury. The twenty-five-year-old accountant stands at over six feet tall and weighs fourteen stone. It was a case of an unstoppable force (Cavanagh) meeting the immovable object (the ground). It was feared in the ground that he had been badly injured. The paramedics took no chances and placed his head in a protective collar before taking him from the pitch and onwards to hospital. Sean Cavanagh is made from stern stuff: it is believed that he was able to join the Tyrone team for the post-match meal that evening!

Above: Michael Ennis unleashes an unstoppable shot to the Tyrone net past John Devine.

This goal in the thirtieth minute came seconds after Sean Cavanagh's nasty-looking injury. A high ball in from Des Dolan was flicked on perfectly by Denis Glennon, and half-back Ennis stole a yard on Tyrone's PJ Quinn to finish to the net. Quinn was to pick up a back injury before the Mayo game but he remained on the panel throughout the campaign. The twenty-one-year-old made an excellent impact in 2008 and he will be an integral part of the Tyrone Senior team in future years. For Michael Ennis, it was his second goal of the campaign and he would receive an All-Star nomination come September. This goal gave Westmeath added belief, but losing two players to red cards was costly. Afterwards Manager Tomas O'Flatharta commented "Discipline has been high, high, high, high on our agenda; it really affected us, even though we were still in the game for a long time afterwards.

Above: Westmeath's captain Des Dolan gives way to Tyrone's Enda McGinley in their Qualifier clash in Omagh.

Judging by the power in McGinley's right arm, it was a wise decision by Dolan to forego the tackle. Westmeath came to Omagh with a half-decent pedigree, fancying their chances against Tyrone. In the semi-final of the Leinster Championship, a crowd of 67,075 watched a disappointing game as reigning champions Dublin made it to their fourth successive Leinster final, with an unconvincing two-point win over Westmeath. Des Dolan top-scored in that game for the Midlanders with five points, three of which came from frees. Dublin subsequently destroyed Wexford in the Leinster final; Westmeath felt that, having run the Dubs so close, they had a chance in Omagh. Despite overcoming Tipperary in the Qualifiers, Westmeath departed the Championship in Omagh.

MATCH 5

Saturday, August 2 – Croke Park

All-Ireland SFC Qualifier Round 3

Croke Park: Mayo 1-9 Tyrone 0-13

Left: Colm McCullagh takes a tumble as he is tackled by Mayo's Peadar Gardiner in the All-Ireland Qualifier at Croke Park.

The Red Hands again just did about enough in their clash with Mayo to come away with a one point victory. They rode their luck, and could easily have been knocked out by the runners-up in the Connacht Championship. In its match report on Mayo's defeat, the *Connaught Telegraph* printed the following obituary to the team:

'Succumbing to an average Tyrone team, bereft of the natural talent and ability that brought the Red Hand County two All-Ireland titles in recent years, Mayo's 2008 championship campaign petered out tamely at Croke Park.'

After the tie, the 'average Tyrone team, bereft of any natural talent and ability' were to show what they were truly made off. The game against Mayo was what players and managers label 'just one of those games'. However, as Kerry – and now Tyrone – have proved over the past number of years, it's all about peaking in late-September. A win on the way – no matter how scrappy – is always welcome.

Right: Behold the King of Ulster Marching to the Sam!

Sean Cavanagh recovered from a nasty-looking neck injury, which he picked up against Westmeath, in time for the Qualifier against Mayo. The man from the Moy had not incurred any serious damage, but younger brother Colm was ruled out of this game after suffering a dislocated shoulder against Westmeath.

Here Sean sprints past Peadar Gardiner, showing the determination that made 2008 essentially 'Cavanagh's Year'. In the weeks after the All-Ireland Final, the accolades for Cavanagh did not stop. As well as a third All-Ireland medal, Sean Boylan named him as the captain of the Irish team that would travel to Australia for the Compromise Rules tournament. It was the fourth occasion on which Cavanagh had been chosen for Ireland in this series. Meath legend Boylan spoke of his decision to appoint Cavanagh as captain: 'Sean Cavanagh has been in the form of his life this year. He was "man of the match" in the All-Ireland final. Sean was one of the key players in Tyrone's march to glory this year. He is an excellent communicator and leads by example on the field. He is also ideally suited to the International game, and it is a tremendous boost to have him on board for the trip Down Under.'

Above: Enda McGinley put in a man-of-the-match performance for Tyrone against Mayo.

Mayo's Tom Parsons can only look on as McGinley is first to the ball. McGinley has been with Mickey Harte for over a decade and served his apprenticeship in Senior football in the watchful shadow of Peter Canavan. He was the vital cog in midfield for Tyrone in 2008. Speaking after the Mayo game, the Errigal Ciaran man expressed his satisfaction with the result:

'It was great to get back to Croke Park and that was one tough game. This will stand us in good stead, and I'm just glad we managed to come out on top. We had good spells in the match and the game could have gone either way. We knew we had to up our game in the second half. It wasn't the prettiest or most flowing football, but that's when it comes down to sheer effort and thankfully we came through.'

Mickey Harte noted after the game: 'Our problem this year is we haven't converted enough of our chances, and we need to nail those chances and inject more fluency in our play'. Dublin were to find out to their cost that Tyrone had indeed worked on the shortcomings to which Harte had alluded after the Mayo clash.

Above: Ryan McMenamin leaves Keith Higgins in his wake as he surges forward at Croke Park.

Mayo footballers are the great under-achievers of this current decade. Twice they have been to All-Ireland Finals – 2004 and 2006 – and twice they have been beaten heavily by Kerry. In 2006 they took a leaf out of the 1984 Tyrone side's book and decided to warm-up in front of 'The Hill' before their semi-final clash with Dublin. Whatever impact it had, it seemed to have affected Dublin: Mayo – who were then managed by Mickey Moran – produced a storming second half to beat the Metropolitans. The Sam Maguire has not been to Mayo since 1951, though the County did collect a Minor title in 1985. In 2001 Mayo made the breakthrough by winning the National Football League crown, beating rivals Galway in the final by a single point. However, Galway had the last laugh that year when they won 'Sam' by beating Meath in the final, while the people of Mayo could only look on in envy.

Right: Davy Harte holds off the challenge of Mayo's Aidan Higgins.

The media in Mayo were particularly scathing of their own side – as well as Tyrone after this encounter. Writing in the *Mayo News*, pundit and former Mayo star Kevin McStay said the following:

'In a game that remained there for the taking for close on an hour or so of average-to-good football, it was a shame we didn't just push on and take it. Two mediocre teams, pale shadows of their last incarnations, huffed and puffed but never convinced they were taking this Round 3 Qualifier game as if it was a matter of footballing life or death. So, Tyrone live to die another day and Mayo troop home with heads bowed once more, their season in ruin due to two single-point defeats'

The words 'So Tyrone live to die another day' were very wide of the mark by McStay. Despite the criticism, Mayo manager John O'Mahony confirmed that he would be staying on as their manager.

Above: Philip Jordan shows his relief as Tyrone hold on to see off the challenge of the Mayo men.

'Tyrone may no longer possess the same class as their previous All-Ireland winning seasons but they showed enough savvy to narrowly overcome Mayo in the second All-Ireland SFC qualifier at Croke Park this afternoon and book their place in the quarter-final.'

So began the *Irish Times* report on the game that Monday. It wasn't pretty, but in the end it was effective. The early stages saw the Red Hands hit points through Davy Harte, Enda McGinley and Sean Cavanagh. Despite this, Mayo soon found their range and Conor Mortimer scored the game's only goal just before the half-hour. By that stage of the game Tyrone trailed by a single point and went in at half-time 1-5 to 0-7 in arrears.

Tyrone then hit six unanswered points after the break to surge ahead by a single point – 0-13 to 1-7 – and held on for victory as two late Mayo frees from Alan Dillon and Conor Mortimer left a single point between the sides. Thirteen points was a lucky total for Tyrone, with Sean Cavanagh top-scoring with four white flags to his name.

Above: Mickey Harte gives the thumbs-up sign to his players after the victory against Mayo.

It was a case of played three, won three in the Qualifier series – the 'one game at a time' philosophy was paying dividends. The Tyrone manager has in the past couple of years dipped his feet into the world of professional boxing, by mentoring the progress of family friend Damien Taggart. Taggart had his first professional fight in the King's Hall in Belfast on the December 2007 undercard of the John Duddy vs. Howard Eastman contest. It was a winning debut for the Omagh man, who had shed over three stones to make the welterweight division. Harte has great motivational powers and the ability to inspire his charges to greatness.

Harte is a master of psychology, but some teams have taken the motivational route to the extreme. In 2008, it was reported that Dublin had distributed a secret 'Blue Book' to their players. It seems that this guide contained motivational quotes from war generals, world leaders and philosophers which were designed to inspire the Dublin players. Needless to say, the Dubs were dumped out by Tyrone in the next round.

MATCH 6

Saturday, August 16 – Croke Park

All Ireland SFC Quarter-Final

Tyrone 3-14 Dublin 1-8

Right: Tyrone and Dublin fans indulge in some 'heated debate'
during their quarter-final tie in August.

Croke Park is an intimidating arena at the best of times, but a
game against Dublin in Headquarters is akin to entering the lions'
den. Hill 16 is a truly awe-inspiring sight with all its colour and
noise. It can intimidate a visiting team but sometimes sides can
be inspired. When Tyrone took on the Dubs in 2008 in front
of 71,000 spectators, the Red Hands totally outplayed the home
side and produced a truly remarkable result. Sometimes, as this
picture illustrates, fans can fail to take a defeat in good grace.
Dublin have consistently come up short in the All-Ireland series
in recent times and Tyrone showed no mercy.

Left: Fisticuffs

"So, how are things up around the Moy?" Tempers flare at Croke Park as Dublin goalkeeper Stephen 'Clucko' Cluxton squares up to Tyrone substitute Ryan Mellon, while Dublin corner-back David Henry looks on. It had been a disastrous day for the Metropolitans as they had capitulated to a superior side in front of their ever-loyal – and patient – fans. Cluxton, who has five Leinster Championship medals and three All-Star awards to his name, had suffered a torrid time as the Dubs failed to make an impression in the later stages of the championship yet again. Ryan Mellon is keeping his cool, happy in the knowledge that the game has been won. The Moy man would go on to win his place on the Tyrone starting line-up for the Final and thus claimed his third All-Ireland medal. His point just after half-time against Kerry came at a crucial time in the match, and stretched Tyrone's lead to three points.

Above: Tyrone captain Brian Dooher shows the determination that brought Tyrone glory in 2008 as he evades Dublin's Tomas Quinn.

Dooher's performance against Dublin in August's quarter-final was truly a joy to behold. The Clann na nGael clubman defied the critics as he went from strength to strength during 2008. Brian's performance against the Dubs that wet August day secured for him the Opel Gaelic Player of the Month Award.

Speaking of the award, the Chairman of the selection committee and former Kerry manager, Jack O'Connor said, "I often hear people describe Brian Dooher as a great old warhorse, but that does him an injustice. For a start, he has too much all-round football skill to be lumbered with that label and in any case, his engine is so dynamic that he could probably out-gallop your average warhorse. His man-of-the-match display against Dublin in the All-Ireland quarter-final smacked of real class. Apart from three delightful points from play, he again showed his natural leadership qualities by repeatedly looking for the ball and opening up the Dublin defence with his powerful, selfless runs. He was also to the fore in the semi-final victory over Wexford, once more underlining his importance to the Tyrone game plan."

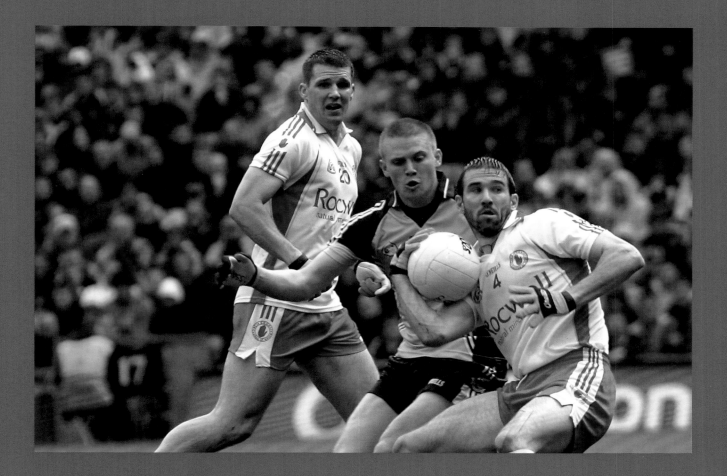

Above: Ciaran Gourley takes on Dublin's Tomas Quinn while Collie Holmes looks on in the rain at Croke Park.

In 2008, Ciaran Gourley brought glory to St Patrick's Academy in Dungannon – where he is on the teaching staff – when he coached them to Macrory and Hogan Cup success. Indeed, several pupils from the school were members of the successful Tyrone Minor side which prevailed after an epic struggle against Mayo in Longford on 27th September. Collie Holmes' season was to change for the better when he was drafted into midfield to partner Enda McGinley prior to the Dublin game. The pair formed an effective partnership and Holmes, the Dungannon Integrated College schoolteacher, was retained for the semi-final against Wexford, and the final against Kerry. Holmes, who plays his club football with Armagh Harps, had spent a lot of time out of the game through injury, but 2008 was to end in sweet success.

Left: Philip Jordan waits to pounce as Dublin's Diarmuid Connolly falls to the ground during their quarter-final tussle.

The Irish summer of 2008 was truly one to forget as the rain fell constantly. The quarter-final tie between Kerry and Galway the previous week became the first-ever Championship match to be played under floodlights as torrential rain fell throughout the second half. The following Saturday, 16th August, was also a poor day for football, but Tyrone settled quickly in the conditions and thrived as the game progressed. Jordan was an integral member of the victorious Tyrone sides of 2003 and 2005 – picking up All-Star awards in both seasons. During 2006, the Moy man missed the season as he was travelling in Australia. He returned to the side in 2007 and picked both Dr McKenna- and Ulster Championship-winning medals. In 2008, he was back to his vintage best in the half-back line.

Derry pundit Joe Brolly suggested that the Tyrone display that day against Dublin was an 'immaculate performance'. For twenty-one-year-old Dubliner Diarmuid Connolly, a Leinster Championship winner's medal was all that the season would deliver, as the Metropolitans thirteen-year wait for All-Ireland glory continued.

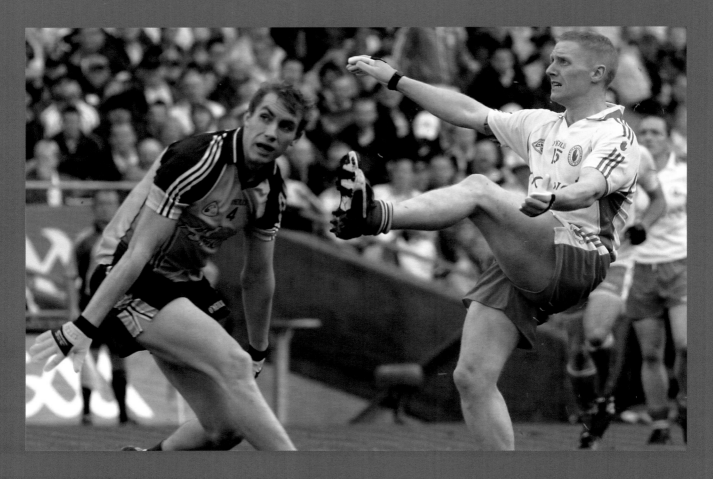

Above: Dromore clubman Colm McCullagh is seen here slotting the ball over the bar against Dublin.

McCullagh was a total revelation for Tyrone in 2008, with many believing that he was the man who made the Tyrone forward line tick. His clever passing ability and positioning sense set up many scores, especially in the Dublin game. The thirty-year-old is a natural footballer and, whilst not a County star at Minor or Under-21 level, he was a panel member in the winning Senior side of 2005. His sporting ability was recognised by Irish League soccer side Newry City, and he was involved with them until 2006. After he left Newry, he concentrated on Gaelic Football and in May 2007 made his full debut for Tyrone in the Ulster Championship game against Fermanagh. McCullagh fired over three points against the Dubs and added four in the semi-final against Wexford. In the final against Kerry, he was limited to a single point. However, the Dromore man had picked up an injury early in the game, and was forced to leave the field in the twenty-fourth minute; McCullagh's exit made way for the return of Stephen O'Neill to the Tyrone side.

Above: Davy Harte bursts through the Dublin defence on his way to hitting Tyrone's third goal of the game, in the fiftieth minute.

Tyrone basically ran at Dublin for the full duration of the game and wore down the Metropolitans' resistance in the process. Davy (a nephew of manager Mickey Harte) provides plenty of options from his roving half-back role, and showed his determination to hold off the challenge of the two Dublin defenders. The pass that made the goal came from Tommy McGuigan, but Harte's composure when finishing past Stephen Cluxton showed his undoubted class. By this stage, Dublin trailed by 1-05 to 3-09, with twenty minutes left. The trickle to the exits on Hill 16 turned into a torrent after Harte's goal, as there was no way back for the Dubs. The Errigal Ciaran man went on to star in the final, where he subdued Kerry's Brian Sheehan and sent over an excellent point in the first half. When Kerry's star-turn Paul Galvin entered the fray in the second half, he was well marshalled by Harte.

MATCH 7

Sunday, August 31 - Croke Park

All Ireland SFC Semi-Final

Tyrone 0-23 Wexford 1-14

Right: The safe hands of Martin Penrose pick out a fellow Tyrone player during the comfortable win over Wexford in the semi-final on 31st August.

The St Davog's of Aghyaran star was one of the famous 'Beardy Boys' of Tyrone and contributed three points to the team's total that day, as the fairy-tale season for Wexford came to an end. Dropped from the starting fifteen after the game against Westmeath, Penrose duly bounced back in the game against Mayo. In the semi-final, Mickey Harte had to make a tough tactical call in the moments before the game when he dropped Brian McGuigan and brought in Penrose at centre-forward. Martin was not found wanting – his contribution that day justified the late change. It was a novel day also for Tyrone supporters as both Minor and Senior teams won at Croke Park to qualify for the final. For Martin Penrose, the victory over Wexford meant that his razor blade was put back in the bathroom cabinet as a final now beckoned. On the day of the final, Harte again was to call on the services of Martin Penrose before the game when he chose him over Brian McGuigan – again neither Harte nor Penrose were found wanting during the game.

Left: Tyrone's Brian McGuigan escapes the attentions of Wexford's Brian Mallon during the semi-final.

Wexford's season in 2008 was one of peaks and troughs. On 1st June, the county staged an inspired comeback against the Royals of Meath to triumph by the bare minimum – 2-14 to 2-13. With twenty minutes left in the game, Meath led by ten points and seemed certain for a Leinster semi-final clash with Laois. The Wexford supporters in Carlow's Dr Cullen Park were to witness an awesome effort from the Model men as a goal by PJ Banville signalled one of the comebacks of the decade. A victory over Laois then saw Wexford face Dublin in the Leinster Final, but they capitulated on a scoreline of 3-23 to 0-9. However, they were not finished and took the scalp of Ulster champions Armagh in the quarter-final at Croke Park. Mattie Forde gave Francie Bellew a proverbial roasting, and effectively won the game with a goal on 61 minutes. The game against Tyrone was a bridge too far for the Model County.

Left: Collie Byrne and Conor Gormley seem to play Gaelic Football without the ball during the semi-final.

Tyrone's relatively easy victory in this game was their fifth successful All-Ireland semi-final appearance. In 1986, the Senior team led by Eugene McKenna saw off the Connacht champions Galway on a 1-12 to 1-9 scoreline. That victory sparked off a mass ticket hunt in the O'Neill county as the tune of 'Come on Tyrone, Come on Tyrone, We're gonna bring the Sam Maguire home' echoed around the county.

After losing to Kerry in the '86 final, Tyrone's next appearance at the semi-final stage in August 1995 saw Galway as their opponents once again. Peter Canavan was the man on the spot as he hit seven points in Tyrone's 1-13 to 0-13 victory. The final that year against Dublin is remembered for Canavan's eleven points and referee Paddy Russell deeming that Canavan had lifted the ball from the ground to score the equaliser – the wait went on for Tyrone. In 2003 Tyrone came to Croker and played Kerry off the field, in a game that changed the face of football tactics. Some pundits did not like the Tyrone style, but nobody in the Red Hand County cared, as Peter Canavan lifted 'Sam' after the defeat of Armagh. In 2005, it was again 'that man Canavan' who placed over the free to send Armagh out of the semi-final by a single point. In the final, Kerry – as in 2008 – were to fall to a more determined and fitter Tyrone side.

Above: Two of the Best in the Business - Messrs Dooher and Morris.

'Captain Fantastic' Brian Dooher shows a clean pair of heels to Wexford's captain Colm Morris. Brian Dooher has been around the Tyrone senior set-up since the 1995 All-Ireland defeat to Dublin. The pain felt by Tyrone that day probably still drives Dooher to greater and higher achievements. In 2008 Dooher, team colleague Sean Cavanagh and Kerry's Colm Cooper were the three players short-listed for the All-Star player of the season award. Dooher's greatest strength is shown in the following: the first question posed by Tyrone's opponents is invariably: 'How do we stop Brian Dooher?'

Wexford were hindered in this game by the loss at half-time of star-player Mattie Forde.

It may well be a cliché, but Matty Forde would walk on to any football team in Ireland. Born in the town of Ballyfad, Forde plays his club football for Kilanerin and is a truly prolific marksman for the Model County. In 2004, he top-scored in both the National League and the Championship, winning an All-Star for his efforts. In 2006 he was truly inspired, as he scored 12 points as Wexford dumped Meath out of the Leinster Championship. However, in the 2008 semi-final Forde (who had been held scoreless) had to retire at half-time due to an Achilles injury. Despite this, Wexford mounted a spirited comeback after the break and found the net through Ciaran Lyng. In the end it was not to be, as Tyrone qualified for their third final in six years, while the Wexford footballers have been waiting since 1918.

Above: The Two Ciarans in Full Flight

Tyrone's Ciaran Gourley tracks the run of Ciaran Lyng as Brian Dooher waits for a breaking ball. The semi-final was a rarity in many terms – firstly it was the first time that the counties had met at this stage and, secondly, the sun was shining. In reality, the Wexford team got to the 2008 semi-final on sheer merit but they had exceeded their wildest expectations for the year, and seemed to lack hunger required. The opening exchanges of the match were close enough but eight unanswered points from Tyrone told the tale of the tape. By half-time Tyrone led by 0-14 to 0-6 and it was essentially 'game over'. However, in the RTÉ studio at Croker, analyst Colm O'Rourke thought that Tyrone would win only by "by three or four points" while the astute Joe Brolly observed it was "strictly business" for Tyrone. To their credit, the Model County men did stage a comeback of sorts in the second half – but Tyrone held firm. Four unanswered points from Philip Jordan, Ryan McMenamin, and Martin Penrose effectively put them back into the comfort zone.

Above: Kevin Hughes and Philip Jordan celebrate after the semi-final victory over Wexford.

The Final is now three weeks away and many nights of hard slog lie ahead. The phones will start ringing and the doors will start rapping with the 'traditional' queries about tickets. The streets of the villages and towns of Tyrone will soon stand bedecked in the red-and-white of the team. One subject will dominate the conversation football and, of course, the old query "Have ye any tickets spare?"

Soon the media will be on the prowl looking for an interview, a juicy snippet, or just a 'wee quote'. The nights will draw in as 21st September approaches, and the floodlights will illuminate the hard work on the training field. The pundits will predict and the tickets will be touted. However, on the evening of 31st August, the Tyrone team will relax and enjoy their victory and let the rest all fall into place.

Above: The fans celebrating another score against Wexford.

The fans of Tyrone have always brought colour to Croke Park and the road to Dublin is a well-worn path for the county's supporters. In the Seventies and Eighties, days out at Headquarters were few and far between. The victory over Armagh in the 1984 Ulster Final – 'the Frank McGuigan game' – created its own momentum and excitement in the county. On semi-final day at Croke Park the Tyrone fans turned out in their thousands to see Art McRory's team face the mighty Dubs. It was the GAA's Centenary Year, and the first time that the two counties had clashed in the Championship: Tyrone went down fighting by 2-11 to eight points. That game was interesting in that the Tyrone side ignored tradition and decided to warm up at the Hill 16 end of the ground before the game – it did not go down well with the 'Jacks' on the Hill to say the least. In 1986, the All-Ireland between Tyrone and Kerry was noted for the mass of colour that the Tyrone fans brought in their tens of thousands to Croker. That day, almost a quarter of a century ago – saw Tyrone fans' hopes dashed by a remarkable Kerry comeback. Leading by three points at the interval, Paudge Quinn got the vital goal for Tyrone and history was in the making. However, what happened after that is still hard to bear for every fan of the Red Hands – and best passed over.

MATCH 8

Sunday September 21st - Croke Park

All Ireland SFC Final

Kerry 0-14 Tyrone 1-15

Left: The picture that will be framed and displayed for eternity in pubs, clubs, shops and houses across Co. Tyrone.

The days of the team shot are long gone and now the panel pose as one on the Croke Park pitch. It is said that the amount of humble pie eaten by Southern journalists in the week after the Final had to be seen to believed.

For a decade, from the mid-1980s to mid-1990s, the pressure on Tyrone to lift 'Sam' was immense and proved to be too much. The County had seen Down take two titles in the 1980s and then neighbours Donegal and Derry made their breakthrough. In 1995 Tyrone must have thought they would never win a Senior title when 'that decision' in the Dublin game cost them dear. Still they persevered, and finally, in 2003, they reached the pinnacle. As 2005 and 2008 proved, they were no one-hit wonder in All-Ireland terms.

Above: Tommy McGuigan gets an unhelpful hand from Kerry corner back Padraig Reidy – who in 2007 became the first player from the Scartaglin club to win a Senior All-Ireland with Kerry – during the All-Ireland final at Croke Park.

Ardboe man McGuigan will go down in history as the man who scored the only goal of the 2008 final. In doing so, he put Tyrone in the driving seat for their ultimate success. Earlier in the campaign, McGuigan had an off-day against Mayo in the Qualifiers but redeemed himself with some exemplary performances in the latter stages. Tommy is, of course, the brother of Brian and Frank Junior, and son of the Tyrone legend that is Frank McGuigan – who could forget 1984? Another brother, Shay, the youngest of the dynasty, was a member of the successful Tyrone Minor squad of 2008. The Kerry side who faced Tyrone had their critics, but mostly the opinion of the pundits was that they were untouchable. Colm O'Rourke said after their defeat of Cork in the semi-final that it was a 'marvellous exhibition' and one that 'restores faith' in the game. Meanwhile, Joe Brolly was a bit more reserved in his praise saying that the Kingdom's forward line was the key to their success against Cork, but noted that their full-back line was at 'sixes and sevens'. This shrewd observation from Brolly was exploited by Tyrone and Tommy McGuigan seconds after the second half began on All-Ireland final Sunday.

Above: Justin McMahon holds off the challenge of Kerry's Kieran Donaghy while Declan O'Sullivan looks on.

Justin McMahon made his mark in 2008 as the dependable full-back in the Tyrone side. A younger brother of Joe, Justin filled the difficult position with a maturity that was an absolute credit to the Omagh St Enda's player. Previously, the full-back position had posed difficulties for Mickey Harte, but McMahon soon brought a degree of security to the rearguard that was crucial in the county's success. In the final, Kerry employed the tactic known as 'Plan A' – i.e. to launch high balls into the 'Twin Towers' of Kieran Donaghy and Tommy Walsh. It was soon apparent that McMahon *et al* were not going to be caught out by this tactic. For Kerry, in the latter stages of the game, there seemed to be no 'Plan B'. Kieran Donaghy and the Kerry forwards had enjoyed field days in the finals of 2006 and 2007; in 2008, their luck ran out. Donaghy's father is from Tyrone, and his mother from Kerry – he spent his early years in Beragh, where generations of his family are associated with the Red Branch Club.

Right: Stevie O'Neill takes on Kerry's Mark O'Sé on the wing.

The return of Stephen O'Neill to the Tyrone side in time for the Final provided a boost to the squad, as well as raising some eyebrows throughout the County. At the start of the year the Tyrone legend decided to retire from inter-County football after enduring two years of serious knee injuries. For the twenty-eight-year-old, who had been awarded the Player of the Year award in 2005, it seemed that he would never represent Tyrone again. However, after the semi-final victory over Wexford, it was announced that O'Neill had made himself available for selection – the players agreed and Stevie was back in contention.

He replaced the injured Colm McCullagh in the twenty-fifth minute. Whilst O'Neill was slightly off the pace of the game, his pass-through which ended in the Tyrone goal showed the class that the fans had come to expect from the star. At the end of the game, he was clearly emotional and had proved again how vital he was to Mickey Harte's team.

Above: Kerry's Aidan O'Mahony challenges Ryan McMenamin during the All-Ireland final.

O'Mahony's pedigree as an astute defender is undoubted in GAA circles. The Garda Síochána from Rathmore in the Kingdom made his inter-county debut in 2004 and claimed his first Championship winner's medal against Mayo that year. In 2006, Kerry again defeated Mayo: O'Mahony's performance that day won him the RTE Man of the Match accolade. In the 2008 final itself, O'Mahony marked Martin Penrose early on and then picked up Sean Cavanagh. Cavanagh frustrated the Kerry back, who was booked in first-half injury time for a foul on the Tyrone star. 'Ricey' McMenamin had a solid game throughout the final, as he effectively neutralised the threat of Kerry's Eoin Brosnan. On 29th September, both McMenamin and O'Mahony were nominated for the Vodafone-sponsored All-Star awards. Tyrone topped the list with ten players in contention for awards, while Kerry followed behind with nine.

Above: Kerry full-back Tom O'Sullivan stretches the rules – and a shirt – as he tries to contain Sean Cavanagh.

They say that Kerry don't really 'try' in the Championship until August. In the semi-final of the Munster Championship, Kerry were flattered in their 1-14 to 0-5 points win over Clare in Killarney on 15th June. The main talking point from the game, however, was the second-half sending-off of Kerry's Paul Galvin. The player then slapped referee Paddy Russell's notebook out of his hands, before arguing with a linesman and his team-mate Tomás Ó Sé. That win saw Kerry through to yet another Munster final, where they would lose to arch-rivals Cork on a 1-16 to 1-11 scoreline. Kerry may well have lost the Munster battle against Cork, but would gain revenge in the All-Ireland semi-final on 24th August with a 3-14 to 2-13 final score. In the early rounds of the Qualifiers, Kerry had a goal to spare over Monaghan while, in the quarter-final against Galway, they had five points to spare in the torrential rain.

Right: Stevie in the thick of the action.

Referee Maurice Deegan was forced into action at the end of the first half as things threatened to boil over between both teams. Darragh Ó Sé, ended up being yellow-carded for an apparent use of the elbow on Sean Cavanagh. The bad grace started a bout of pushing and shoving among the players which continued after the half-time whistle was blown. One of the Kerry officials was caught up in the melee below the Hogan Stand and was unceremoniously upended. The game itself, despite a couple of high tackles, was not considered to have been a dirty game. When it came to composure and sticking to a gameplan, the Tyrone team won hands down. Firm in their defending and ruthless in attack, Tyrone finished with a flourish and hit five unanswered points to win the game.

Right: The moment when men became legends and history was made.

The final whistle on All-Ireland Final Sunday signals a mass invasion of the Croke Park turf from members of the Tyrone panel. Caught like a rock in a swollen river of glee is the figure of Tyrone's Assistant Manager Tony Donnelly. The Augher man has been Mickey Harte's right-hand-man throughout the glory days of the 2000s. Donnelly co-managed St McCartan's to Tyrone championship glory in the 1980s, and was associated with the Tyrone minor sides that flourished under Harte. His stunned demeanour contrasts starkly with the joy around him – perhaps the moment would take that bit longer to sink in for the man whose contribution to Tyrone football has been immense over the years. The Croke Park official to the right is set to break the magical spell that has entranced Tony Donnelly.

Above: The jubilant Tyrone goalkeeper Pascal McConnell is embraced by trainer Fergal McCann just after the final whistle.

Pascal was called upon at the last minute to replace first-choice goalkeeper John Devine, owing to the sudden death of his father, John Devine Senior, on the day before the match. On the afternoon of the final itself, the Tyrone side wore black armbands as a mark of respect to Mr Devine and 82,500 spectators observed an immaculate minute's silence before the throw-in. Pascal McConnell made several crucial saves during the game, including one from Tommy Walsh and the late goal bound effort from Declan O'Sullivan, which could have won the game for Kerry. Afterwards, Pascal paid tribute: "I cannot speak highly enough of John Devine. He is just a fabulous guy. It's great to dedicate that win to him."

Pascal was between the posts for Tyrone in the 2005 final, while Devine had been the custodian in 2003. From Newtownstewart, Pascal is of course the younger brother of the other Tyrone goalkeeping legend Finbar.

Above: Brian McGuigan and Mickey Harte embrace below the Hogan Stand.

In the dressing room before the final, Mickey Harte had the unenviable task of breaking the news to Brian McGuigan that he would not be starting the game, despite being named in the team. The same fate befell Ciaran Gourley in the dressing room. It was a heart-breaking moment for both manager and players, but it says so much for the esteem in which Harte is held that the decision was accepted in the interests of the Tyrone cause. The respect that each member of the Tyrone squad has for Mickey Harte is unquestionable. His record speaks for itself: an All-Ireland Minor title in 1998 was followed by three Senior titles, not to mention three Under-21 titles also. Add to that two Ulster Senior titles and a National Football League title in 2003 and it is a truly wonderful record. Winning All-Ireland titles takes more than coaching and tactics – it is also a mixture of determination, pride, hunger and faith, with skill, power and fitness thrown in. Mickey Harte has instilled all these qualities into his teams.

Above: The Holy Trinity of Tyrone football.

From left to right: Mickey Harte, Tony Donnelly and trainer Fergal McCann. His role in Tyrone's success may not be as prominent as Messrs Harte and Donnelly, but McCann's contribution as trainer has been crucial in bringing Tyrone continued success. McCann was a mere spectator in the Hogan Stand when Tyrone won their first All-Ireland in 2003, but he has looked after the fitness of the squad in the successful years of 2005 and 2008. A native of Augher, Fergal's role has been to condition the players to the peak of their fitness before they take to the field. Crucially, in the last ten minutes of the final, it was evident that the Tyrone players had the edge over Kerry in terms of fitness. The oldest man in the Tyrone squad was Brian Dooher at thirty-one years-of-age, yet the inspired running performances of the 'Miracle Man' in 2008 bore testament to McCann's ability as a fitness coach.

Above: Mickey Harte holds aloft the 'Holy Grail' of Gaelic Football: The Sam Maguire Cup - or just plain 'Sam' to his friends.

Harte is happy (and why not?). He, personally, had to endure some stinging comments from a section of the supporters – and of course the media – after his team's defeat to Down in the Ulster Championship, so this moment was as sweet as could be. The trophy is not an original and is known as the 'Son of Sam'. In 1928, Kildare captain Bill 'Squires' Gannon became the first man to lift 'Sam'. However, in the mid-1980s, the GAA agreed to have a replica made and the 'son' was born. It was a Tyrone man, Dr Pat McCartan, from Carrickmore, who chaired the committee which was charged with finding a suitable commemoration to GAA stalwart, Sam Maguire, who died in 1928. Based on the design of the Ardagh Chalice, Hopkins and Hopkins of O'Connell Bridge made the cup at a cost of £300. The Son of Sam now knows the highways and by-ways of the O'Neill county like the back of his hand. Tony Donnelly awaits his turn.

ALL IRELAND MINOR FOOTBALL

FINAL REPLAY

Venue: Pearse Park, Longford

Saturday 27th September, 2008

Tyrone 1-20 Mayo 1-15

Left: Just when you thought that things couldn't get any better – 'Tom' joins 'Sam' in Tyrone.

Tyrone Minor captain Ronan McNabb pictured with the Tom Markham Cup. Tyrone were denied a rare double at Croke Park on All-Ireland final day when their Minor team drew with Mayo in the Minor final. In the replay in Longford the following Saturday, the Minors made no mistake when, after extra-time, they triumphed over their opponents by 1-20 to 1-15.

In 1980 Kerry had been the last county to achieve this rare double, and it was a fitting ending to a truly brilliant season for the Red Hand County. In the space of a decade, the county has secured nine All-Ireland titles – three Senior, two Under-21 and four Minor.

The replay was a truly titanic battle with Tyrone getting the upper hand after a tiring second period of extra-time. Things were still in the balance with three minutes left when Tyrone got a penalty. Peter Harte took his point from the spot, and then Niall McKenna's effort finally ended Mayo's dreams in Longford.

Above: Tyrone's Peter Harte is pursued by Mayo's James Cafferty

After an epic first match at Croke Park, Tyrone's teenagers had five points to spare over a gallant Mayo side. Kyle Coney – who is Australia-bound – hit three points, which helped Tyrone to a 8-6 half-time lead. Mayo surged back and with fifteen minutes left they held a slender one-point lead. Tyrone equalised at the death with a point from Niall McKenna. In extra-time, Tyrone hit an unanswered 1-3 – the goal coming from Conor O'Neill. It was too much for Mayo and, despite James Cafferty's goal, the Red Hands were home.

Tyrone's mighty Minors lifted the County's seventh All-Ireland Minor title, and after the glory of 21st September, it was the icing on the cake.

Above: Kyle Coney – Star Player with Australian Dreams.

Five points from play in the Minor final replay earned Kyle Coney the Man-of -the-Match accolade. The eighteen-year-old from Ardboe's O'Donovan Rossa club announced in the week following the game that he would travel to Australia, to try his hand in Australian Rules football. The offer of a two-year deal from the Sydney Swans club attracted the youngster and, despite pleas to stay at home, he was adamant that he was to go to Oz. Coney signed a two-year 'Rookie' deal with the Swans in July and senior star Sean Cavanagh, apparently, met with him to ask him to reconsider the move. There is no doubting

Coney's pedigree as a Gaelic footballer. He scored some vital points in Tyrone's campaign and set up the equalising score for Mattie Donnelly in the drawn game. He has proved to be a versatile and strong-willed player, and was immense in Tyrone's win over Meath in the semi-final. A trip to Australia will see him follow in the footsteps of Martin Clarke, Down's 2006 Minor star, who joined AFL side Collingwood.

Left: Ciaran Girvan of Tyrone passes the ball to Conor O'Neill as Mayo's Shane McHale comes in to tackle.

Let's be realistic. This year's Tyrone Minor side was one of the most talented squads ever assembled. Much was expected from – and delivered by – the team, since its backbone contained several of the Dungannon players that won the All-Ireland Colleges title in 2008. They eased their way to the Ulster title and then accounted for Roscommon and Meath to get to the final.

After the heart-stopping draw in the first game against Mayo at Croke Park, there was added pressure on the team to deliver the goods. The County was in a state of ecstasy after the Senior team's win, but manager Raymond Munroe kept his players focused:

"We'll make history if we win, but I think the most important thing is that the fellows focus on winning the game of football. The historical facts will take care of themselves after that."

Munroe had moulded a side that had everything. From their movement and distribution, to their skill and fitness, everything was top-drawer. In the end they also had hunger, and that was crucial. Success has now become natural in the Red Hand County, and future years will hear a lot more of the Tyrone Minors of 2008.

Above: A bit of a regular sight these days in Aughnacloy – Tyrone arriving back with their old friend 'Sam'.

On the Monday after the epic final, the Tyrone team left Dublin bound for the O'Neill County. The first port of call was the town of Aughnacloy on the Tyrone-Monaghan border. The proud GAA folk of Monaghan must be envious, as their near-neighbours have now passed through the county three times with 'Sam' in tow. Thousands of happy fans packed Aughnacloy's Main Street as the team entered on an open-top bus just before seven o'clock. Brian Dooher and Mickey Harte then led the team onto a hastily-erected stage to resounding cheers. Captain Dooher paid tribute to the fans for their loyalty in 2008:

'On behalf of this Tyrone team, I would like to thank you for all your support throughout the year. Early on in May, things did not look so good, but thankfully the boys stuck at it. It is really hard to believe we are back here again, and we have a lot of people to thank for it, Mickey Harte amongst others.'

It was a late night for the squad as a stop in Ballygawley was made before the team arrived in Omagh.

Above: Mama we're all Beardy Boys now! A happy family await the Tyrone team in Aughnacloy.

The Tyrone 'Beardy Boy' phenomenon caught the imagination of the GAA public in 2008. Many rumours were circulated as to why the beards were grown – but, be it 'for luck' or 'for a laugh' it certainly had people talking. Another rumour circulated that Mickey Harte had one night related the Biblical story of the bearded Samson who acquired his strength due to the fact that he had never shaved or cut his hair – so the Beardy Boys decided to follow his example to gain extra strength. From dressing room pacts to fashion accessories, the newspapers churned out acres of print on the Tyrone beards. Where they modelled on ancient Celtic warriors, Woodstock veterans or reclusive hermits? The answer is that the Beardy Boys had us stumped.

Why will Santa Claus not be welcome in Kerry this year?

Kerry people are fed up with bearded men wearing red and white.

Above: A snapshot of the legions of fans who had gathered in Omagh to greet their heroes.

Many thousands of Tyrone fans were denied a ticket for the final by the arrangements which the GAA put in place for its yearly football showpiece. Tickets are distributed among the 'great and the good' of the Association and forwarded to every County Board and then clubs throughout Ireland. The competing counties are given a nominal amount – which is totally inadequate for the numbers who wish to purchase a ticket. The sad fact is that a scramble takes place, with genuine fans losing out through, in many cases, sheer bad luck. The real fans – those who stood in the wind and rain watching the team in February or March – can miss out on the biggest game of the year. Unscrupulous touts can ask – and get – exorbitant prices for tickets in and around Dublin on the Final day itself. The growth of the internet has allowed this practice to be carried out online – and many fans are ripped off.

Above: The Leaders of Men – Brian Dooher and Mickey Harte hold the Sam Maguire – the Cup that most definitely cheers.

Messrs Dooher and Harte parade 'Sam' in front of their enthusiastic followers at Healy Park in Omagh. Born in 1952, Mickey Harte was until recently a schoolteacher at St Ciaran's Vocational School in Ballygawley. Harte's love of Gaelic Games was nurtured at Omagh Christian Brothers' School and he represented Ulster at Colleges' level in the 1960s. He attended St Joseph's Teacher Training College in Belfast (known as 'The Ranch'). From 1975 to 1982 Harte represented Tyrone Seniors, and was on the losing side in the 1980 Ulster Final when Armagh took the title. As a teacher at St Ciaran's he guided his pupils to many honours on the football field, including a vocational All-Ireland title. Errigal Ciaran was established in Ballygawley in 1990, and Harte's excellent record as their Underage manager soon brought him to the attention of the Tyrone County Board. The rest is history as Minor, Under-21 and Senior All-Ireland titles have travelled Tyrone's way in recent years.

GAA FOOTBALL ALL STARS 2008

The GAA All Star football awards for 2008 were a triumph for Tyrone. Seven players from the squad received accolades – the same number as in 2003, but one less than the tally for 2005.

The Magnificent Seven from Mickey Harte's side were: Brian Dooher, Conor Gormley, Justin McMahon, Davy Harte, Philip Jordan, Enda McGinley and Seán Cavanagh.

It could be believed that many other members of the Tyrone side were somewhat unfortunate not to have been included in the final list. However, some pundits argued that the ability of many of Tyrone's team to play anywhere on the park hindered their chances of landing an award in a particular position.

Tyrone's All-Ireland final man-of-the-match Sean Cavanagh and Kerry defender Tomas Ó Sé, collected their fourth awards, while Tyrone's Conor Gormley, Philip Jordan and Brian Dooher all landed their third awards. In 1980, Kevin McCabe made history by becoming the first Tyrone man to land an All-Star accolade.

The Vodafone GAA Football All Stars 2008

Goalkeeper:
1 Gary Connaughton (Westmeath)

Full-backs:
2 Conor Gormley (Tyrone) All Star '03, '05
3 Justin McMahon (Tyrone)
4 John Keane (Westmeath) All Star '04

Half-backs:
5 Davy Harte (Tyrone)
6 Tomás Ó Sé (Kerry) All Star '04, '05, '07
7 Philip Jordan (Tyrone) All Star '03, '05

Midfield:
8 Enda McGinley (Tyrone)
9 Shane Ryan (Dublin)

Half-forwards:
10 Brian Dooher (Tyrone) All Star '03, '05
11 Declan O'Sullivan (Kerry) All Star '07
12 Seán Cavanagh (Tyrone) All Star '03, '04, '05

Full-forwards:
13 Colm Cooper (Kerry) All Star '02, '04, '05, '07
14 Kieran Donaghy (Kerry) All Star '06
15 Ronan Clarke (Armagh) All Star '06